D0518118

LAKE ONTARIO

A TRUE BOOK

by

Ann Armbruster

Children's Press®
A Division of Grolier Publishing
New York London Hong Kong Sydney
Danbury, Connecticut

Reading Consultant
Linda Cornwell
Learning Resource Consultant
Indiana Department of
Education

Subject Consultant
William D. Ellis
Editor of the quarterly journal
of the Great Lakes
Historical Society

A boat on Lake Ontario

Library of Congress Cataloging-in-Publication Data

Armbruster, Ann.
    Lake Ontario / by Ann Armbruster.
        p.   cm. — (A true book)
    Includes index.
    Summary: Discusses the history, nautical stories, and industrial and
social significance of Lake Ontario.
    ISBN 0-516-20014-3 (lib. bdg.)   ISBN 0-516-26105-3 (pbk.)
    1. Ontario, Lake (N.Y. and Ont.)—Juvenile literature. [1. Ontario,
Lake (N.Y. and Ont.)] I. Title. II. Series.
F556.A76 1996
974.7'9—dc20   96-2081
                                                                   CIP
                                                                   AC

Contents

Grooves carved by glaciers filled with water to form the Great Lakes.

The Smallest Lake

The United States and Canada are two countries in North America. Thousands of years ago, huge glaciers covered this area. When the glaciers melted, they left behind five freshwater lakes between the United States and Canada. Today, these

Minnesota

LAKE SUPERIOR

C
A

O
N
T

Mich

igan

Wisconsin

LAKE MICHIGAN

LAKE HURON

Illinois

Indiana

Ohio

LAK

U
N
I
T
E
D

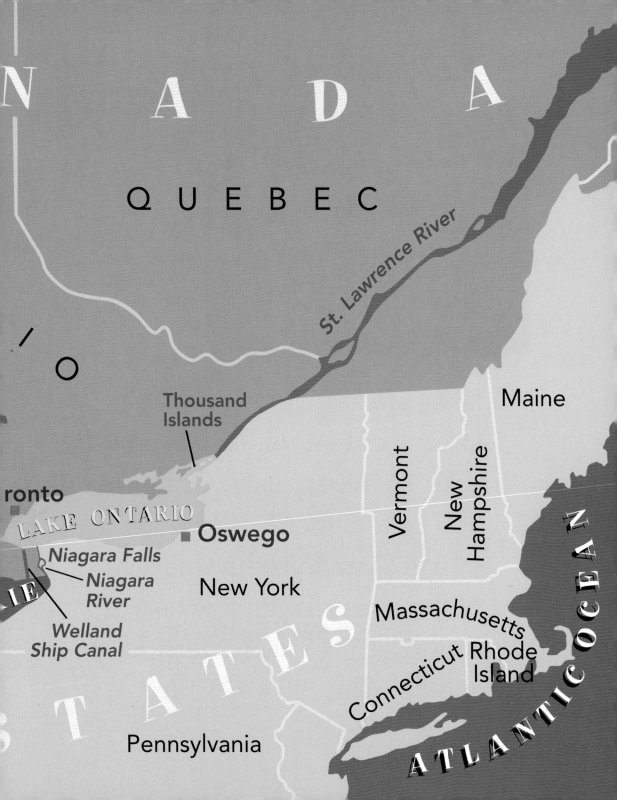

People fishing on the shores of Lake Ontario

lakes are known as the Great Lakes—Lake Erie, Lake Huron, Lake Michigan, Lake Ontario, and Lake Superior.

Lake Ontario is the smallest of the Great Lakes. It is only 193 miles (311 kilometers) long and 53 miles (85 km) wide.

The Gateway Lake

The Great Lakes are an inland waterway that form a kind of stairway from the Atlantic Ocean to the middle of North America. Lake Ontario is the gateway to the other Great Lakes.

Lake Ontario empties into the Atlantic Ocean through the St. Lawrence River. It is an

Ships carry cargo from the Atlantic Ocean to the Great Lakes. In this picture, ships dock in Toronto harbor.

important link in the St. Lawrence Seaway, which is a waterway that links all five Great Lakes to the Atlantic Ocean. It is also the first Great Lake a westward-bound ship will travel after leaving the Atlantic Ocean.

Iroquois Indians

Europeans first reached the Americas about five hundred years ago. At that time, hundreds of tribes of American Indians lived there.

Five Indian nations occupied the land south of Lake Ontario, now known as New York State. The five Indian nations were the Mohawk, Oneida, Onondaga,

This early French map shows the location of the Five Iroquois Nations (Les Cinq Nations Iroquoises) around Lake Ontario (Lac Ontario).

Cayuga, and Seneca. The Europeans called all five groups the Iroquois.

Each Indian nation had its own territory. Generally, the Iroquois built several villages in forest clearings. They also built sturdy stockades for protection against their enemies.

War was the way of life for the Iroquois. A warrior's reputation increased with each battle. Fear and hatred were common feelings. Through the 1400s

The Iroquois met in councils of war (left). The Mohawk Indians used weapons such as knives and tomahawks (below).

and 1500s, the five nations fought each other.

At one point, the nations formed the Iroquois Confederacy to strengthen them against enemies. Later the Tuscarora Indians joined them. Peace replaced their warring way of life.

In the 1700s, the British and the French fought each other for control of North America in the French and Indian War. Most of the Iroquois nations sided with the British, and

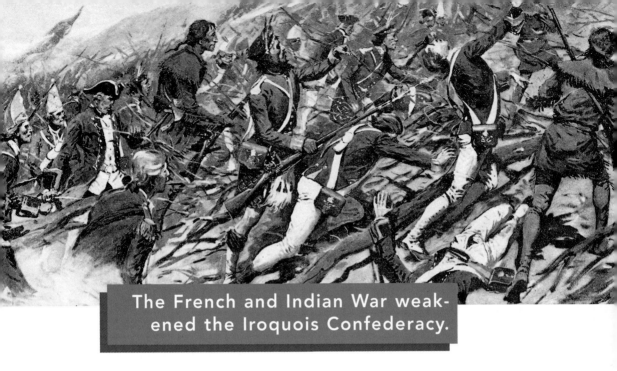

The French and Indian War weakened the Iroquois Confederacy.

some sided with the French. This weakened the Iroquois Confederacy.

Over time, the Iroquois were pushed onto Indian reservations. Today, most of the Iroquois live on reservations in New York State, and in Ontario and Quebec in Canada.

Reservations

During the early and mid-1800s, the United States claimed American-Indian lands as their own. The government made peace treaties with the Indians, but soon broke the agreements. The government forced Indians to move from their homes to areas of land set aside for them, called reservations.

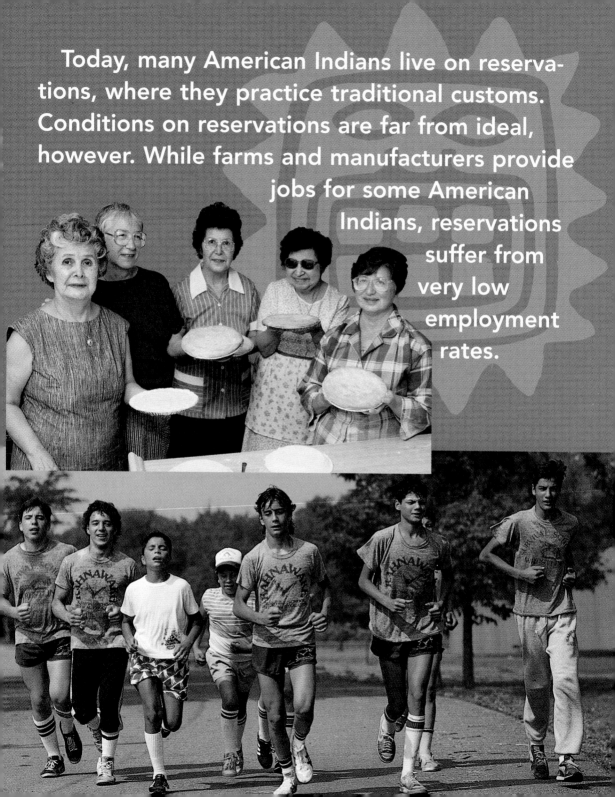

Today, many American Indians live on reservations, where they practice traditional customs. Conditions on reservations are far from ideal, however. While farms and manufacturers provide jobs for some American Indians, reservations suffer from very low employment rates.

Ships of the Great Lakes

The Great Lakes gave people freedom to travel long distances by water. Swift birchbark canoes were the first form of transportation on the lakes.

The *Griffon* was the first sailing ship on the lakes. In 1679, the tiny sailboat made only one voyage before it disappeared in a violent lake storm.

American Indians paddled their canoes (left). The *Griffon* used sails for power (above).

The second sailing ship was the *Oswego*. Then *Walk-in-the-Water* became the first ship to combine steam power with sails. By 1755, the British were building battleships in the Lake Ontario region. At that time, the British and

French fought for control of the Great Lakes area.

In 1888, Alexander McDougall invented a boat of unusual design. It looked like a whale floating on the top of the water, so it was named the "whaleback." Later it was

A whaleback boat in the Soo Canal

nicknamed the "pigboat" because the ship's bow was snout shaped.

Most of the ships on the Great Lakes are freighters. These sturdy boats carry millions of tons of goods through the Great Lakes and St. Lawrence River. Their cargoes consist of coal, lumber, cement, iron ore, and grain. The tanker is a special type of freighter. It is designed to carry oil and other liquid products.

A freighter carries cargo through Lake Ontario (left). Dock equipment lifts heavy cargo from a ship (above).

On most freighters, cargo is loaded and unloaded by dock equipment. Some ships have elevators that can transport three levels of automobiles at one time!

23

People watch as a freighter passes.

Today 1,000-foot (305-meter) boats carry cargo through Great Lakes waters where American Indians once traveled in dugout canoes.

The Ghost Ship

By 1776, the British were fighting colonists in the Revolutionary War (1775–1783). Great Britain kept a large naval force on the Great Lakes. One of their most powerful warships was the *Ontario*. This 80-foot (24-m) ship could challenge any American ship on Lake Ontario.

In October 1780, the *Ontario* set sail for Oswego, New York, carrying British soldiers and military supplies. A fierce storm hit the Great Lakes. The *Ontario* was never seen again.

Later, settlers found British soldiers' caps in the waters of Lake Ontario. More than seventy soldiers and seamen were lost.

Thousand Islands

The Thousand Islands are a group of small wooded islands that dot the St. Lawrence River and the eastern end of Lake Ontario. American Indians called the area "the place where the Great Spirit lives."

An exact count of these islands has never been made,

The Thousand Islands are clustered at the eastern end of Lake Ontario.

but estimates range from 1,700 to 2,000. Some islands are only large enough for one small tree!

In the early 1900s, American millionaires built summer resorts on many of these islands. One wealthy man built a ninety-eight-room palace called Casa Loma. His home still stands today.

A house barely fits on one of the smaller islands (below). The grand Casa Loma (inset) stands on a larger island.

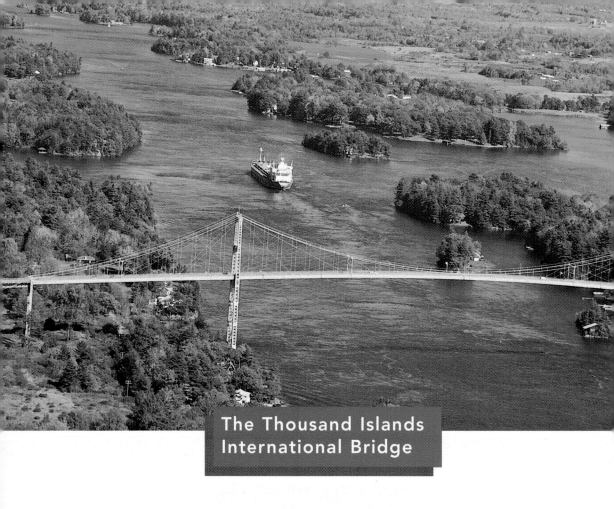

The Thousand Islands
International Bridge

The Thousand Islands
International Bridge connects
some of the larger islands.
The bridge is 6.5 miles (10.5
km) long.

Niagara Falls

The Niagara River connects
Lake Erie to Lake Ontario.
But before the water reaches
Lake Ontario, it drops 326
feet (99 m) over Niagara
Falls.

   Niagara Falls is actually two
waterfalls. The Horseshoe
Falls are on the Canadian side

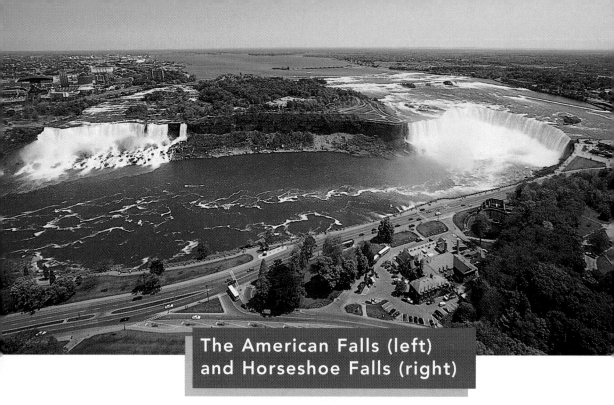

The American Falls (left)
and Horseshoe Falls (right)

of the U.S.–Canada border.
The American Falls are on the
U.S. side.

The overflow from Lake
Superior, Lake Michigan, Lake
Huron, and Lake Erie feeds
the falls. About 40 million

gallons (151 million liters) of water rush over the falls every minute.

Ships sailing on the Niagara River must bypass the falls via the Welland Ship Canal.

Water rushes over Niagara Falls.

Dangerous Stunts

What is the strangest way a person can become an instant celebrity? How about riding over the Niagara Falls in a barrel? Four people have ridden the falls on purpose and lived. Annie Edson Taylor was the first. On October 24, 1901, she climbed into an oak barrel and rode over the falls. When she climbed out at the bottom, covered with bruises and cuts, she said, "Nobody ought ever to do that again!"

Welland Ship Canal

The Welland Ship Canal is one of the world's greatest engineering projects. It provides a flat waterway between Lake Ontario and Lake Erie so that ships can travel around Niagara Falls.

This amazing waterway is 27 miles (44 km) long and

300 feet (91 m) wide. It has seven large locks that lift or lower ships 327 feet (100 m). These locks can handle ships up to 730 feet (223 m) long.

The Welland Ship Canal in 1928 (above) and an aerial view of the canal today (right)

A gate leads ships into a lock on the canal (left). The Welland Ship Canal opened industry between Lake Ontario and the other Great Lakes.

The Welland Ship Canal is an important part of the St. Lawrence Seaway. It opened up industry between Lake Ontario and the other Great Lakes.

Toronto, Ontario

Toronto lies on the north shore of Lake Ontario. The name Toronto is an American-Indian word meaning "meeting place." In earlier times, Indians used the area as an overland route between Lake Ontario and Lake Huron.

Today, Toronto is the capital of Ontario and one of

People sailing in Toronto harbor (right) can see the skyline of Toronto, Ontario (above).

Canada's busiest ports. The city is the center of Canadian industry. Most of Canada's publishing, television, and film production companies are located there.

Railroads in Toronto (top) bring goods to all parts of North America. Freighters on the St. Lawrence Seaway (bottom) travel from the Great Lakes to the Atlantic Ocean.

Toronto is also a major trans-portation center. Manufactured products of the region are sent to all parts of the world by railroads and airplanes. In addition, ships transport goods via the St. Lawrence Seaway.

Lake Ontario Today

Lake Ontario is the gateway to the Great Lakes. About five million Canadian and U.S. citizens live on and around its shores. Campgrounds and resort communities add to the beautiful scenery. The fertile land south of Lake Ontario produces great

Peaches (above) and apples (left) are grown south of Lake Ontario.

harvests of apples, peaches, and grapes.

Lake Ontario has been threatened with widespread pollution. Recently, regulations and strict water-quality standards have been introduced. Both the U.S.

and Canadian governments enforce these new standards. Lake Ontario is cleaner today. Environmentalists and citizens must do their best to keep it that way.

People enjoy boating on Lake Ontario.

To Find Out More

Here are more places where you can explore Lake Ontario and the states and provinces around it:

 **Books**

 **Organizations**

Fradin, Dennis Brindell. **New York.** Children's Press, 1993.

Granfield, Linda. **All About Niagara Falls.** Morrow Junior Books, 1988.

MacKay, Kathryn. **Ontario.** Children's Press, 1992.

Murphy, Wendy, and Jack Murphy. **Toronto.** Blackbirch Press, 1992.

Sherrow, Victoria. **The Iroquois Indians.** Chelsea House Publishers, 1992.

Great Lakes Commission
400 Fourth St.
ARGUS II Bldg.
Ann Arbor, MI 48103-4816
(313) 665-9135
glc@glc.org

New York State Department of Economic Development
Division of Tourism
1 Commerce Plaza
Albany, NY 12245
1-800-CALL-NYS

Ontario Travel
Queens Park
Toronto, Ontario
Canada M7A 2E5
1-800-ONTARIO

 **Online Sites**

Tour Lake Ontario

http://www.great-lakes. net:2200/places/watsheds/ ontario/ontario.html

Discover the endless attractions of the Great Lakes Circle Tour. This online site has facts about Lake Ontario, including information about conservation efforts around the lake.

Visit Ontario, Canada

http://www.great-lakes. net:2200/partners/GLC/pub/ circle/ontario.html

On Ontario's Great Lakes and St. Lawrence River shores, you can visit parks and see baseball, museums, and wildlife. Tour Toronto, Hamilton, Niagara Falls, and more.

Explore New York

http://www.great-lakes. net:2200/partners/GLC/pub/ circle/newyork.html

Travel the New York Seaway Trail, a 454-mile (730-km) route along Lake Erie, the Niagara River, Lake Ontario, and the St. Lawrence Seaway.

Facts and figures about the Great Lakes

http://www.great-lakes. net:2200/refdesk/almanac/ almanac.html

Includes information about populations and the region.

Niagara-on-the-Lake

http://www.niagara.com/ chamber.notl/

Niagara-on-the-Lake is just a few miles from the famous falls, with a history and attractions all its own.

Important Words

birchbark bark of a birch tree

bypass to go around an area by another way

glacier large mass of ice formed when snow piles up and does not melt, often up to 1 mile (1.6 km) deep

lock boxlike space that raises or lowers ships as they travel from one water level to another

naval relating to the navy

stockade protected area formed by poles stuck into the ground

territory area belonging to a certain group of people

Index

Meet the Author

Living in Ohio, close to the Great Lakes, Ann Armbruster pursues her interest in history. A former English teacher and school librarian, she is the author of many books for children.